A Special Gift

for

Karen Liebner

with congratulations
for graduating from

Pioneer High School

Class of 98

Presented by

The Harvey Family

Letters from
the College Front

Letters from the College Front

Girls' Edition

Lisa Hutchcraft Whitmer
Ronald P. Hutchcraft

BAKER BOOK HOUSE
Grand Rapids, Michigan 49516

Copyright © 1993 by Baker Books
a division of Baker Book House Company
P.O. Box 6287, Grand Rapids, MI 49516-6287

ISBN: 0-8010-9722-3

Sixth printing, December 1995

Printed in the United States of America

Produced by The Livingstone Corporation.
James C. Galvin and Daryl Lucas, project staff.

To
My loving, godly husband **Rick**
Your love and leadership light up my days!

Mom and Dad
Thank you for your commitment to Jesus and to each
other.

Aunt Val, Doug, and Brad
Thanks for being not only family, but also close friends.

Contents

Note to the Reader

In 1492, Columbus accidentally found the New World. He really didn't mean to—he was actually looking for something else. Unfortunately, there was no one to ask for directions. No one from his country had ever been there before to even know directions!

High school is now your Old World. Soon you'll be setting sail for the New World of college.

I wrote these letters to "Jessicas" everywhere, because I wanted them to have a map for college. Usually it's not polite to read someone else's mail, but in this case, I hope you will. These letters come from someone who has seen the New World of college.

After each of my letters, you'll see some additional comments by my dad. He has been serving as a great navigator for me, my brothers, and a lot of other people our age for thirty years. He's an experienced map-maker.

You may never have a day named after you like Columbus did, but with a map you can reach the destination you're heading for. I pray this book will be a good map for you as you navigate the waters of college. Thanks for picking it up!

And have a fun year at school!

Your friend,

Lisa

It's Here!

Dear Jessica,

"Prepare for landing." As our plane neared Chicago, I knew I wasn't just landing on a runway, but entering a whole new stage of life! This wasn't just another family vacation that I'd return from in a few days—I was rapidly approaching my new home for the next four years.

What a day we chose to move me to college! It was pouring rain. All landing gates but one were closed, and because of the severe weather our plane was the last one allowed to land. I had never heard of an international airport being paralyzed. We got to the baggage claim area. What chaos! There were people and bags everywhere. We quickly learned that our own ride wouldn't be picking us up because of the terrible flooding. Well, the radio programs my whole family came out to Chicago to record this weekend would have to wait, too. We were flooded in at the airport!

We managed to gather together all of our—excuse me, all of *my*, as my brothers would say—luggage, and form "Camp O'Hare." Ten bulging suitcases and two trunks (with heavy tags) later, I found myself perched on top of my life! I'd always been known to pack a lot for vacations, and my brothers would groan under the weight of my suitcases, but this really was embarrassing.

Actually, I did seem to have the best seat in the airport, and I had a lot of time to think about this new transition I was going through. My two football-playing brothers went off in search of "Pizza! Pizza!" . . . Mom headed off to make some phone calls . . . and Dad went in search of beds for five people at the quickly-filling-up hotel. I was left alone with Mt. Luggage.

As I sat on top of all the earthly possessions I brought to school—clothes, yearbooks, pictures of my boyfriend from home, cassettes, plus all the stuff girls can't do without!—the word *college* began to sink in. My high school life began flashing before my eyes—striving to get good grades, filling out college applications, participating in extracurricular activities, going to Youth for Christ events, spending time with friends. . . . It dawned on me that this word *college* I'd heard all through high school was really here.

Suddenly I realized I was at a major crossroads of my life, heading into the unknown while sitting on top of all that was familiar to me.

You're about to head into all this a few months from now—same huge packing job, same feelings, same wonders and worries. I have survived these beginning days, but maybe it would be nice for you to have a road map from somebody who's already been down the same road. I'll keep in touch.

Jess, I hope you choose a nice dry day to move to college. And you might only want to pack two suitcases and one trunk . . . but I'll hire out my brothers to help you move if you'd like!

Your "sis,"

Lisa

Perms aren't.

Sure, the hair stylist says all that kinky hair is a perm. But ask how long the curls will last. "Oh, two or three months." Now wait a minute—that's not a perm . . . that's a temp!

Today you stand on top of a mountain that took you twelve years (or longer?) to climb—Mt. Senior. And from that vantage point, you can see what most people in high school miss . . . the difference between what's "temp" and what's "perm."

The big party, the big game, the big crush—they all look very temporary as you look back from Mt. Senior. The perms? The lives of people for whom you made a difference.

I think there ought to be a "Make a Difference" yearbook. It wouldn't be like the classic yearbook, with your smiling picture and a list of your activities. "Soccer 1, 2; Chess Club 4; Nintendo 3, 4; Central Detention 1, 2, 3, 4." No—those are temps. Instead this yearbook would show your picture and next to it a list of the people who would say, "You made the difference for me." That's permanent.

You don't have much time left before you say good-bye to all your high school friends—many of whom you'll never see again, unless you take them to heaven with you. In these closing days on Mt. Senior, be sure you have told your friends about Jesus and how they can know him. They may or may not listen. They may file the information away and come back to Jesus later in life. But you won't have to live with the regrets of letting them go without letting them know.

Mt. Senior actually gives you a view in two directions—not just looking back at high school, but looking ahead at that next exciting mountain. Ahead of you is Mt. College and one of life's priceless moments . . . a NEW BEGINNING.

Leave your high school masks in high school. Decide the "you" that you want to be before Day One of college ever hits. Take an honest look at the weaknesses and bad habits that tended to trip you up over the past four years, and get them under control now.

In fact, the months or weeks between Mt. Senior and Mt. College are a time to get your life under control. There will be plenty of craziness to handle in college. Take these "in between" days to get you together.

And no matter how you decide to wear your hair, concentrate on the perms.

Ron

College Food
and College Fat

Dear Jessica,

Flab. That word strikes terror into the heart of every American girl! Not big thighs and sit-ups!

While I've been gaining new knowledge here at school these first couple months, I've also been gaining some new pounds. It's been great having a variety of foods around, but let's just say the scale is not my best friend right now.

During orientation week, the upperclassmen warn you about the dreaded "freshman fifteen." I think the guys warn you because they don't want to date girls with pimples and love-handles. And the girls warn you because they know it's so easy to gain the weight and so hard to get rid of it!

Part of my downfall has come because of the *huge* selection and abundance of food in the dining hall. How many moms can actually cook three different hot entrees, have a deli sandwich bar nearby (in case you don't care for the entrees), five incredible desserts, various unlimited beverages, fresh-baked muffins each morning, a huge salad bar, soft frozen yogurt and ice cream, plus twelve different kinds of cereal to choose from for dinner just in case the reheated turkey tetrazzini doesn't look too appetizing? As I was saying, the choices of what to eat (and the *quantity!*) have been endless!

Unfortunately, mealtimes aren't my only opportunities for food. There are so many opportunities to *socialize* with new friends—going out for ice cream, fast food restaurants, and the Student Union, to name a few.

Another downfall is that my roommate and I have a small refrigerator in our dorm room. It's great to keep cold sodas on hand, but a few other not-so-diet foods have crept in there to satisfy my snack attacks. Don't laugh, but the first time I really felt "independent" and grown-up here at school was ordering my first Domino's pizza with my roommate! I didn't even have to ask Dad if we could send out for pizza—I could just decide and call up the delivery guy myself! This fun new habit turned into just that . . . a habit. Studying late at night with nothing to eat, still a hundred pages to read about Descartes' reasoning pertaining to sociological philosophy (?!?), and my stomach screaming for something to munch on! So . . . pizzas and other junk food snacks helped me through many a long studying night, but now I have some tight clothes.

No, you don't have to panic and go to aerobics school. You can still go to college, but here are a few suggestions that might help. Before you get to school, make sure you do some kind of regular exercise. It'll really help to be in good shape when you get here.

When you get to college, remember to stay active so those dreaded "thunder thighs" don't surprise you! As a freshman, the *only* advantage to not being allowed to have a car on campus is that you walk everywhere—built-in exercise! But I've found out that's not enough to burn off those pizzas.

Fortunately, the college doesn't just give you a huge selection of food and no way to burn off the calories. They have some exercise equipment available (even if you're not into a sport), like bicycles and a swimming pool. (Don't just sit in the whirlpool—swim laps!) Plus, some upperclass girls lead aerobics, where you pay a certain fee, but get some money back if you go to all the sessions (good incentive, huh?). But make sure you schedule exercise—otherwise you won't do it, and you'll notice that horrible word creeping up on you (I'll whisper it): *flab*.

It really can be fun to exercise at school because you have new friends to go on walks with, bike with, and swim with, not just *eat* with! Find other fun ways to socialize.

Also, during those late-night studying times, I'm learning that fresh fruit, yogurt, popcorn, or granola bars make great snacks. You'll also have more energy (and more money from not tipping all those pizza delivery guys) if you exercise regularly and eat better.

Be careful of the other extreme of weighing a few extra pounds. Being too obsessed with food can also lead to anoxeia or bulimia. Don't damage your body permanently. Seek *balance* with eating and exercising.

I have to run! (Actually, I'm going swimming!) Those pizza calories gotta go!

Your "sis" with a weakness for pizza,

Lisa

A Word about College Food and Fat

"And . . . in this corner . . . weighing in at 210 pounds . . . Round Ron Hutchcraft!"

That's how they could have introduced me my first day at college. At only five feet eight inches tall, I was the original blimp.

And it didn't feel very good. I entered my "new beginning" feeling self-conscious about my weight. I was anxious to meet all those new girls, but not sure they would want to meet me.

I learned a lesson late that I hope you learn early—enter college in the best physical shape you can. Get your body under control before you enter Appetite City.

Appetites often rule people in college. It was meant to be the other way around. You will self-destruct if you don't control the college appetites that scream, "Feed me! Sex me! Sedate me!" In the Bible, the apostle Paul says the one who "gets the prize" is the one who "goes into strict training." Paul even went so far as to say, "I beat my body and make it my slave" (1 Cor. 9:24–27).

So learn to say no to that body of yours. If your body is under control when college comes, you'll be ready for the social opportunities . . . and ready for an intense load of responsibilities.

If you're carrying an intense load of Twinkies and Big Macs around your middle, dump it now. Don't eat after 5:30 at night, weigh yourself regularly, exercise at night, go to bed hungry, anticipate "pig" times by losing so you can gain without damage. And once you get your weight off, set a weight boundary and never cross it. When you get to it, reverse all engines!

There's a danger, though, in all this weight-control talk— that a "figure obsession" will lead you into anorexia or bulimia. Keep your balance . . . slavery to an eating disorder is more damaging than extra pounds.

If your appetites, your hormones, and your glands run you, you'll be a slave all through college. So make sure your body knows who's boss before you take it to Appetite City.

Ron

Hitting the Books

Dear Jessica,

I got one. That word I heard so much about senior year in high school and didn't quite understand is now sitting in front of me. At first it seemed kind of cool because it said I had no homework due for four weeks! My little friend that dictates how I spend my time: the syllabus.

I can't believe it. In high school I really didn't have to spend much time studying. I got most of my homework done in class and study hall and then enjoyed my afternoons. The only study hall now is an around-the-clock dorm room or library. There's no one to check up on me to see whether or not I'm doing my work, which seems great, but boy! I've been sunk a couple times already!

Have you ever tried to speed-read the Old Testament in one night? What a mistake. When I tried to, the next morning during my final exam I was so confused between Joshua, Joseph, and Jehoshaphat, that I had no idea who was thrown into a pit by his brothers! Plus, the other day I was horri-fied—I actually kept dozing off during a major exam because I had pulled my first "all-nighter"!

Now I always thought "all-nighters" would be fun—but let me just dwell for a moment upon the subhuman feeling you have all day after an "all-nighter." Instead of styling your hair, the curling iron is left untouched in the bathroom as you rush out the door, throwing your drooping locks up into a pony-tail. Terrible feelings of nausea haunt you all morning because your stomach isn't used to staying awake all night eating pizza and junk food. I've heard about people dying in avalanches in the Alps, but even if you stay up all night in an avalanche of studying, you still have only eight hours to get all your work done.

I've lost a lot of sleep over the issue of studying in college (excuse the humor, it was a late night last night). However, I've had to make some major changes just so I can survive until Christmas break (like limiting late-night talks with my roommate!).

First, I now realize that this syllabus-thing really is my friend. It's a guideline for the whole semester. If you think of it, you could spend a chunk of time working really far ahead, and then you wouldn't have any more work for the semester! (I wonder if anyone's ever really done that?) Even though realistically I only have three or four hours "scheduled" for classes during my day, I've had to sit down and make sure studies are a high priority. When I wake up, it often looks like I've got lots of free time, but I've had to schedule study times.

Also—I know, I know, I sound like a teacher or your parents—but one practice that will actually buy you more time is ORGANIZATION! How you manage your time is really how happy you'll end up being with your grades and everything else in life.

Something that has helped me organize my life a little better is to have a clean, organized desk. I got one of those little desk things that holds paper clips, rubber bands, and pens—it sure beats that little plastic box I used to carry to school with rulers and bubble-gum smelling erasers in it. Plus, it's also been good to actually file some important papers and notes in the filing cabinet Mom and Dad bought for me orientation week.

Another wise move is to make sure you study somewhere without distractions. Even the library can be too social a place with people whispering, goofing off, and snoring (no joke!). Now I know this sounds difficult, but turning off music and the TV is a big step to more effective studying. Your study time can be cut in half when you settle down to study in a place where you can fully concentrate.

My next major tip is go to class. That sounds rather ridiculous, but actually, if you miss one day of class, it's hard to catch up! One college class day probably equals one to two weeks of high school classes.

High school studying is very different from college studying. Forget the forty-five minutes of conjugating French verbs and the five algebra problems you had for homework. In college, you'll have to make the most of available time slots to read and go over notes. I've found a lot of time for studying while waiting—for example, for lunch at the dining hall, for a professor to arrive for class, or for a special appointment. (One time I even read some class notes while waiting for a date!)

Make sure you really know the material for your classes. Pure memorizing could get you an *A* in high school, but not always in college. Make sure you really *understand* why those little white mice in psychology respond to electric stimuli the way they do.

About your weekends: Enjoy them while you're in high school (just kidding!). Seriously though, in order to have a free weekend, you've got to capture time during the week for studying. And it's not a bad idea to review some notes before classes again on Monday.

I know you're probably sinking lower and lower in your chair as you keep reading, but I hope some of this can help you make the most of your time when you get here. I wish I had listened or learned sooner some ideas about how to be consistent and organized with studies. And it will pay off—

you'll want to put your grades on the fridge to display them instead of hiding them in your desk drawer.

Off to hit the books, your "sis,"

Lisa

A Word about Studying

It's the most dangerous bus on campus—it has run over more students than any other bus. Greyhound? School bus? No—it's the bus you will board the first day of every class . . . the SYLLABUS.

Make friends with your syllabus. It's your professor's day-by-day description of what you'll be expected to read, write, and report on that semester. Those who do what the syllabus says ride that bus to college success. Those who don't get run over by it.

The big difference between high school and college is that you are expected to manage your own academic life. No teacher nagging you to do it, no heavy-breathing parent standing over you. Your map is that syllabus. Plan your life and your time by it.

If you manage your study life well, you'll win yourself a lot more freedom to do things you want to do. Here are some simple "how's":

1. Learn it in class. Most people attend the class and plan to learn it later. Why waste that time? Listen 100 percent . . . concentrate . . . ask about what you don't understand.
2. Take excellent notes, underscoring what the prof emphasizes.
3. Review new material the same day. Try to make it yours right after you have heard the lecture on it.
4. Do the worst first. It's great for morale to get the most dreaded job out of the way.

The Bible sums up the secret of championship studying: "Whatever you do [being in class, taking notes, reviewing], work at it with all your heart, as working for the Lord, not for men [the professor or your parents]" (Col. 3:23).

So does this 100 percent approach make you a slave to your studies? No! It makes you the boss . . . and it makes you free!

Ron

Parents

Dear Jessica,

What a crazy schedule here at college! Trying to find time to sleep, study, socialize, eat, have fun, and even brush my teeth can be hectic! Something else I've had to make sure I keep a part of my schedule is staying in touch with my parents. It's not as easy or convenient to communicate with them now that I'm miles away.

You're probably thinking, *What do parents have to do with college other than paying the bills?* Now let's just remember those dear people who cleaned up after us as infants, who took care of us during sickness, who put the clothing on our backs, who chauffeured us for years to activities, who . . . (OK, you can wipe the tear from your eye). Basically, they got us where we are today.

Of course, your relationship with your parents really changes between high school and college. Depending on how much you relied on Mom or Dad to do your laundry or fix anything that broke, you could have a rough time adapting to "life on your own" in college. What's even worse is when you're sick. If you grew up like I did, you're probably used to chicken-noodle soup and some motherly T.L.C. when the flu bug bites. No such luck here! (Realize that your roommate and dorm or floor supervisors are not your mother; they're not paid to bake birthday cakes for you or to shower compassion upon you in the middle of the night when you're vomiting.)

A big change in college is that you're no longer part of a family unit on a daily basis. For some, that might be a dream come true; but for others who were real close with their parents and siblings, it can be a struggle to adapt.

Most parents hear from their "freshman-in-college children" about one topic: money. Actually, the topics that parents probably want to hear most about are grades and friends (including any interesting *guys!*). I'm sure that the U.S. Postal Service and long-distance phone companies across the nation make most of their money from desperate college freshmen who contact home requesting help or money from their parents! (I'm sure the concept of calling home collect was developed specifically for broke college freshmen.)

Poor parents. Their child has embarked on an exciting, new adventure in life at college, and the most they hear about is their child's pathetic finances. Make sure you *communicate* with your parents about *life* at college. Some of my friends set aside one hour every Sunday night to write a letter home. Others (like me!) enjoy calling home to give a "life-at-college" update. But whatever you do, be careful! Your parents might have a sudden heart attack if you surprise them by not even mentioning the M-word (money)! Let them know about friends, classes, what the food is like in the dining hall, and even that cute guy you've been studying with! They know you're becoming more independent, but when you take time to include them in your New World, you say "I love you" to them in a loud way!

Going home to visit parents on breaks can be different, too. You've been taking charge of some areas of your life they used to take care of, and they still see you as their little girl. You don't have to regress into acting like a kid, but it is all right to let Mom do your laundry—you'll have to do your own the rest of your life, and it still makes her feel needed! Remember, not only are you in a transition time, but so are your parents! Their nest is becoming a little emptier (or even totally empty). Keep developing a friendship with them—they're great friends to have for life!

Fortunately, parents can also communicate to their college freshman child through special gifts, such as care packages. Joy fills the heart of a broke and hungry freshman when she learns there is a care package waiting for her at the college post office! Most colleges also have some kind of organization through which parents can order birthday cakes, goody baskets (that are delivered during exam weeks), or other special treats. If your parents aren't aware of such a service, you can anonymously drop something in the mail to them about it—maybe they'll get the hint!

Don't forget your parents when you get to college, and actually, while you're still in high school, work on having a healthy relationship with them—it'll make things easier when you move away to college. Also, a smart idea is to talk with them about your expectations for college—share your goals with them, and find out from them what their expectations are for you. It'll make the road at college much smoother if you work to understand each other *before* getting there.

Gotta go—I have to call Mom and Dad collect and ask for some money (just kidding!) and tell them about this great guy I met the other day!

Your "sis,"

Lisa

Amputation is painful . . . especially if it's your son or daughter who's being cut off.

Mom and Dad have sort of gotten used to having you around for eighteen years. Then one day you and your stuff are gone. You go to a New World full of new people and experiences. Your parents stay in the Old World, missing being a part of your days.

It's an adjustment. But it doesn't have to be an amputation . . . if you don't let your new busyness cut you off from Mom and Dad. So . . .

- Don't become a stranger. Keep them up-to-date on your rapidly changing life. If you don't, they will have a hard time understanding you at a time when you really need them. Besides, you need their outside perspective. "Keep your father's commands and do not forsake your mother's teaching. Bind them upon your heart forever" (Prov. 6:20–21).
- Don't just use them as your personal rescue squad. Your parents' number is not 911. It's not much of a relationship if you only call when you're choking financially, expecting them to jump out of the ambulance with a checkbook and administer financial CPR.
- Don't fill up your breaks with everybody else. They count the days until you're home. Save a little time for them.
- Don't expect them to cancel the Family Constitution for you. When you come home, you're going to have to adjust to some expectations and restric-

tions you don't have at college. Your parents need to adjust to your new independence, too. When there's conflict between your freedom and their expectations, talk it out . . . agree on some compromises.

God's command to honor your father and mother is for life. When you get married or financially independent, obey is not the issue anymore. But honor is always there.

So don't let your evacuation be an amputation. Treat Mom and Dad with respect, and you may graduate again . . . from just being their kid to actually being their friend.

Ron

"Your Mother Doesn't Live Here!"

Dear Jess,

Ironing, laundry, and cleaning bathrooms. Yup, I know that wonderful triad of activities ranks pretty high with us girls. Wrong!

I have a distant, vague memory from orientation week when some sophomore showed me where the laundry room was in the basement. But to be honest (as Thanksgiving quickly approaches!), I haven't spent much time there. Yes, I've been wearing clean clothes—but only because at fall break I lugged all my dirty clothes from the first nine weeks of school home with me halfway across the nation for Mom to do.

Now, I *do* know how to do laundry, but being your own mother here at college *does* take time. Unfortunately, even with the tuition we pay, the college does not provide laundry or ironing pick-ups from our doors, like fancy hotels. So, enjoy the luxury of having your mom do your laundry for you for your last few months at home.

Fortunately, there are no dishes to be loaded or emptied out of the dishwasher here—they *do* pay people to do that. But doing laundry, ironing, cleaning the bathroom, and other "mom" jobs will take some time—so you need to make sure you schedule time to get them done. You don't want to lose your new friends because they're scared of the new bacteria cultures growing in your bathroom or of your dirty pants mysteriously crawling across the floor. One advantage to waiting for a while to do laundry is that when you want to get laundry collected, you simply whistle and it all gathers at your feet!

It is important to keep your room picked up on a regular basis, because it's not just *your* room. You *do* live with another human being now, so be considerate. At home, I had free rein of where I wanted to drop my clothes and when I wanted to pick them up, but now we have *three* girls living in *one* room, so I've had to learn to keep my things picked up. Someone once told me this is good training for getting married someday because if you get married, then you'd have to live with a life-long "husband roommate"!

In high school, I always had a "back-up alarm clock" in the morning known as Mom and Dad, but now I realize, no, the college does not provide wake-up calls either. Unfortunately, college is not some glorified hotel. I've had to learn to make sure I don't keep hitting snooze in the morning, no matter how late I was up the night before, because no one but me is going to make sure I'm up to get to class on time!

I recommend becoming acquainted with the laundry room before your dorm room is quarantined by the board of health! You'll need to buy laundry detergent (probably for the first time!), and make sure you have enough quarters on hand (no, laundry isn't free either). If you haven't already, learn some pointers from Mom on how to separate different colors and fabrics, and then make time to do your laundry!

It really isn't that difficult, and actually, think of how awful it is for most *guys* at college, because most of them have *never* done laundry! (I learned that doing laundry was actually a way to make some friends—teaching some desperate guys how to make sure all their white socks don't turn pink!)

One tidbit of info: Saturday mornings are usually a pretty crazy time to do laundry because *everyone* does laundry on Saturday! My suggestion is to do a load of laundry in the afternoon or evening as you're studying. That way you can get it out of the way and have a great weekend and clean clothes too! Also, you might want to get ahead by ironing a few shirts and skirts, so as you rush off to class in the morning, you don't have the added pressure of ironing clothes.

Enjoy having your mom to lean on while you're in high school, but you might want to ask her to jot down some important laundry or cleaning hints before you become your own mother at college!

Your "sis" turned mother,

Lisa

A Word about Messes

"We didn't pay any attention."

That's how the soldier described the reaction to classes on chemical warfare during boot camp. But the interview with him was taking place on the border of Saudi Arabia and Kuwait on the eve of the Persian Gulf War. Things had changed. "They're teaching us about chemical warfare again. Man, are we paying attention now!" Of course! With Saddam Hussein's chemical weapons just over the border, they knew they would need that information.

For you, the freedom and responsibility of college life are just over the border. Yea! And, uh-oh! There are lots of everyday skills you haven't paid much attention to before, but now you need to know them. You're almost on your own!

So eliminate a lot of college stress . . . and be sure you can answer yes to questions like these before you kiss Mom or Dad good-bye:

- Do I know how to make and live on a budget?
- Can I manage a checkbook?
- Do I know how to do laundry? Ironing?
- Do I know about oil changes, tune-ups, changing a tire, and all the other things it takes to keep a car running?
- Do I know how to save money on phone calls by calling at cheaper times of the day and not using the expensive operator-assisted calls?
- Do I know Mom's grocery-store savings tricks?

Maybe you've never paid much attention to life's basic survival skills before. Pay attention now. There's little time to learn them once the battle begins.

Ron

To Drive or Not to Drive

Dear Jessica,

You know how independent you felt when you finally got your driver's license? Well, as a freshman in college it doesn't matter *what* that slip of paper says—I have no car, and I have no way to get off campus except a bicycle and my own two feet. Now, feet and a bicycle aren't that bad . . . except when it rains or snows (winter just began two weeks ago!), or when you have to buy some things at the store (which seems twenty miles away when you're carrying heavy grocery bags!).

Each college has different policies as to whether or not freshmen can have a car on campus. Most schools just don't have enough parking space for every student to have a car. That's why many colleges allow only upperclassmen to have these treasured sources of independence and freedom. Leaving campus becomes a novelty and a long-anticipated experience. Absence and deprivation do make the heart grow fonder . . . and desperate!

When a lady picked me up for church last Sunday, she was somewhat distracted by my playing with the automatic door locks, but what a thrill—I hadn't been in a car for so long! Rides to church, the grocery store, fun activities, and home during school breaks are sometimes pretty hard to come by for freshmen.

A couple weekends ago was really fun because one of my roommates brought her car to school and kept it off-campus for a couple days—what a treat! We made sure we stocked up on food from the grocery store . . . we went to the mall

. . . we went to events far away . . . we went out driving just for fun!

A couple suggestions on how to deal with not having the luxury of transportation at your fingertips. Don't get so desperate you borrow other people's cars—there have been some not-so-happy people (and parents) after a car has gotten dented or cracked up by a friend. You don't want to be indebted to a friend for life, paying off bills just because you wanted to go get Twinkies or pizza!

Some colleges provide rides to grocery stores and malls on Saturdays and times close to holidays (like now, with Christmas coming). That's a great help, and you can learn to plan it in your schedule as some fun socializing time too, when you go with friends or meet new friends along the way!

Some upperclassmen with cars do have sympathy for the campus-landlocked freshmen, and they offer rides to the store or offer to pick things up for you.

If you *do* have the privilege of having a car on campus your freshman year, help others out when they're out of laundry detergent or toothpaste. (Ultimately, *you* might suffer from the odor if your roommate runs out of deodorant!) But remember, you can quickly become a popular access to freedom when people know you have a car. Your prized possession can become a thorn in your flesh when everyone comes begging, and you have studying and sleeping to do! Plus, there's a lot of work and money (for gas and repairs) that goes into taking care of a car. Mom and Dad aren't around when you don't know how to be "Jane Mechanic." And unless you bump into some cute guy who's a whiz with cars, has no studying to do, and who has a heart for helpless girls—you're stuck with a heap of malfunctioning metal!

Enjoy your driving privileges now . . . and you might want to invest in a skateboard for college. But hey, you'll know at least one sophomore with a car at school next year!

Your hitchhiking "sis,"

Lisa

A Word about Transportation

Poor Gilligan. He and his friends were trapped on that island for years.

That "trapped on an island" feeling sometimes hits you in college. And a car is your S. S. Minnow with which to escape.

But whenever you're looking at the car option, don't just look at the pluses . . . there's a price tag, too. Here are three mistakes to avoid:

1. *Underestimating the cost. Cars have to be fed, bathed, fixed. They can make an already tight college budget melt down.*
2. *Underestimating the line at your door. Just when you're trying to figure out managing your time, the "I need a ride" line forms outside your room. It's nice to be needed, but this much?*
3. *Underestimating the temptation. Studies have shown that students with cars generally don't do as well academically. Frankly, a car can be a "Fatal*

Distraction" and a temptation few can handle. It's just too tempting to say "yes" to your wheels and "later" to your homework. If you do have a car, use it as a reward, not an escape. Don't play until you've finished your work.

Focus—that's what College: Year One will require. You need to stay on the island and master living there. Be careful of having a car to escape in. . . . That car could end up sinking you.

Ron

Secular or Christian?

Dear Jessica,

Hey, I hope mid-terms are going well. Christmas break will be a big relief and vacation for all of us!

Thanks for your last letter—college post office boxes can get real lonely. Thanks for giving mine some company! I know you wrote about how your friends in Campus Life and youth group are having a hard time choosing between a Christian and a secular college. It can be a tough decision, but I'll try to answer some of your questions.

Going to either kind of school has advantages and disadvantages. As a Christian at a secular school, you are a bright light in a dark world. Obviously, there are more non-Christian friends to share Jesus with.

At a secular school, your faith and what you believe will really be tested by your professors, friends, and studies. You will find most people are either hostile or unsympathetic toward what the Bible says about serving Christ. Many students and professors at secular universities have lots of sophisticated academic knowledge but have reckless, destructive lifestyles. For example, one of my high school girlfriends who went to a secular college was appalled to wake up many nights to find her roommate sleeping with her boyfriend. In this setting, you won't have your parents or Christian friends around to lean on for support. But taking a stand for Jesus Christ can really strengthen your faith.

Some of your Christian friends might think: *Well, it's no big deal going to a secular college. After all, I'm at a public high school and made it through OK.* There is a *huge* difference between going to high school on a daily basis with your friends and *living* day and night with people who live immorally. I've already heard from some of my Christian friends at secular schools that it's easy to conform because the pressure is so strong.

Premarital sex, drugs, and drinking are all much greater temptations at a secular college. Make sure your faith is really strong before moving into that kind of environment—don't let your light for Jesus grow dim over time.

My dad has always told me: "Satan works by erosion." When you and I would go to the Jersey shore for Youth for Christ conferences, we could see the beach erode away a little more each year. Some parts of the beach aren't strong enough to withstand the constant battering of the waves. Don't let Satan wear you down with the constant assault you'll get at a secular school when you stand for Jesus.

There *are* other Christians on secular campuses, but you'll need to seek them out through churches and the different Christian organizations that exist for college students. Ask around about InterVarsity, Campus Crusade, or Bible studies that can become an important support group for you.

What do Christian colleges offer? The actual environment of a Christian school will be much different because of the people there, plus there will probably be some guidelines that secular schools don't have. But, not everyone at a Christian school is radically committed to Jesus Christ. There are still underlying problems at Christian schools—like drinking, premarital sex, and often a disrespectful attitude toward authority (which includes God!). Plus, the music you hear coming from dorm rooms often is no different from music you'd hear on a secular campus.

BEWARE: Something I've noticed about several people here at school is that there can be a dangerous sarcastic and critical attitude toward God, the Bible, families, professors, friends, studies, the "outside world," and every area of life! It's easy to see that this attitude has resulted in a loss of genuineness and passion and, ultimately, a loss of love for Jesus. I don't completely understand this cynical attitude among students *and* sometimes even faculty. Decide *now*, while you're in high school, to remain strong and pure throughout college. It's not easy to rise above negative influences—even at a Christian college.

Another danger at a Christian school is that many students are just "going through the motions" of Christianity. It's easy to join them, too. Keep your faith *growing* and vibrant. Don't join the huge ranks of stagnant Christians—there need to be more students who are radically committed to Jesus Christ! God doesn't need any more lukewarm Christians—he needs more people like you, Jessica, to live a "no compromise" life for him! When you get here, keep your enthusiasm for knowing Jesus and for reaching out to others who don't know him. You're making a huge difference in high school—don't let that die at college!

I hope telling you about what I've experienced and what I've learned from Christian friends at secular schools can give you a clearer picture as you start to decide where to spend four very important years of your life. Decide *now* that you will *not compromise* in your life wherever you go—whether to a Christian or secular school. It's easy to fall into compromise at either place.

I chose to attend a Christian college because, after attending public high school, I believed it was important for me to get quality Christian training that would prepare me for life. At a Christian school, you still learn the same subjects you would at a secular school, but your professors present the *bib-*

lical perspective and may even pray before class. I also have some older Christian role models I can seek counsel from on various issues. I hope my faith becomes stronger here after four years, because I know these are important training years.

Perhaps some of the best advice I can give you is some my mom and dad gave me as I grew up: "Go M.A.D.!" Go make a difference! Wherever you go to college, *you* go make a difference for Jesus Christ! Don't conform to either environment at secular or Christian schools—*you* have the greatest message to share. And I've found it's the most exciting way to live!

See you next week over Christmas break!

"M.A.D." for Jesus,

Lisa

A Word about Choosing Between Secular and Christian Colleges

I'll bet you didn't know you were so popular. When you became a senior, your mailbox started to explode with college mail. You have probably been contacted by everyone from Aristotle Engineering to Zephaniah Bible College. Isn't it great to be in such demand—and so confused?

In this blizzard of possibilities, you have to sort out one of the most life-shaping choices you'll ever make: "Shall I go to a secular or a Christian college?"

No matter which you choose, you'll have opportunities to enjoy and dangers to avoid. At a secular school, you won't go to the party as people did in high school—you'll live at the party. A Christian college won't be like going to church so much as living at the church.

If you live at the "party," you can go to pieces spiritually. If you live at the "church," you can go to sleep.

You're not just choosing a place to study a major . . . you're choosing your environment and relationships for the next four years. Yes, it is an important decision—one that you and God need to work on together. As you weigh your options, keep the following questions in mind.

If you're considering a secular school, ask yourself:

1. Will I choose Jesus' uniform from Day One at college? You cannot "serve two masters" (Matt. 6:24)—wear the jersey of one team and the helmet of the other. You'll never make it if you don't go publicly, totally Christian right from the kickoff.
2. Am I a "debriefing" person? You will be bombarded every day with godless ideas and lifestyles, and you'll need to be the kind of person who talks through it with another believer. Otherwise, you will just soak up the lies until they erode your faith.
3. Did I stand consistently against the dark pressures in high school? If you didn't stand by Jesus in the part-time darkness of high school, how will you stand in the full-time darkness of a secular college?
4. Will I immediately connect with God's family at my school? God has His kids everywhere—your first

mission is to find the Christians and Christian groups at your school. Following Christ is a family affair, not a Lone Ranger experience. At a secular college, more than most any other place, "let us not give up meeting together, . . . but let us encourage one another" (Heb. 10:25).

God is looking for some dedicated disciples to make a powerful difference for Him in a secular college—and maybe He's sending you. If Jesus assigns you to be His lifeguard there, just be sure you're strong enough to avoid getting dragged under.

Now if you're considering a Christian school, ask yourself:

1. Am I more concerned with what pleases Jesus than with what most Christians are doing? Because the sacred gets so familiar, a lot of students get cynical about what God calls holy, or they get careless or rebellious or hard. If you tend to look to Christians more than Christ, you'll probably catch terminal sleeping sickness.
2. Do I tend to get close to Christian friends who are serious about Jesus? A Christian college is not heaven, or even close. The people who go there come in the same flavors as those in your youth group. So under the word Christian will be everything from spiritual radicals to spiritual rebels. Your choice of friends will make the difference between a Christian coma or a Christian conquest. "He who walks with the wise grows wise, but a companion of fools suffers harm" (Prov. 13:20).

41

3. Will I find a personal mission off campus? Disadvantaged kids to tutor . . . evangelizing teenagers . . . lonely senior citizens . . . an outreach coffee house—it's exercise that will keep all that Bible-banquet from turning to fat. A mission will keep you awake and sharp.

As you make your college choice, remember that you have three basic assignments from God for these next four years:

1. To develop your God-given gifts "to the max."
2. To make a Jesus-difference in the place God sends you.
3. To establish the network of relationships and views on which you will build the rest of your life.

You need to ask your Lord, "Where can I do that best?" Offer him a blank piece of paper to write His plans on. "Trust in the LORD with all your heart and lean not on your own understanding; in all your ways acknowledge Him, and He will make your paths straight" (Prov. 3:5–6).

Secular or Christian? Ironically, the bottom line is the same both places: Does your Christianity consist of you and your environment . . . or you and Jesus?

Ron

Sexual Pressure

Dear Jessica,

Thanks for your last letter—I look forward to hearing from you at home! You mentioned how senior year in high school carries a lot of pressures, along with all the privileges of being at the top of the mountain. In particular, you talked about how many of your friends are giving in to sexual pressure from their friends. If you think staying pure sexually is hard during high school, it can be just as bad, if not worse, in college. Here there is even less of an "accountability factor" than in high school.

Fact number one is that God made us with strong sexual desires—it's *his* plan to keep the human race going, plus to have people enjoy the gift of sex *he* gave them. Fact number two is that God wants sex to be enjoyed within the fence of marriage. No, he isn't some spoilsport. In fact, God *made* sex (not Hollywood TV and movie producers!). It was God's idea in the first place! Fact number three is that the inventor of something knows best how to work it. Can you imagine the game of baseball if its inventor, Abner Doubleday, hadn't established any boundaries and rules? It would be chaos! The same goes for sex—God designed it, and he knows best when sex should occur—within certain boundaries and certain guidelines. For *our* benefit and protection.

Remember: *How* you use your time in college is totally up to you—there's a lot more freedom here than in high school. There's no Mom and Dad watching and checking up on you to make sure you're doing the right thing. More often than not, there's no one to hold you accountable for your actions except yourself. *You* are the one who is personally responsible to God for your decisions. Therefore, before you get to college, it's a good idea to re-evaluate your guidelines for dealing with sexual pressure. There sure won't be anybody else telling you what to do—*you* have to believe that standing firm and deciding to save sex for marriage is the right choice.

Draw physical boundaries now, *before* you get in a compromising sexual situation. Forget trying to decide what's right during a passionate moment—decide *now*, when your hormones aren't running a hundred miles an hour! Also, as girls, we can really help out the guys by watching what we wear—low necklines and high hems really can make it hard for guys to keep their thoughts pure. Be sure to discuss the physical boundaries of your relationship with your boyfriend—*before* temptation strikes.

Since sexual pressure is everywhere, make sure you plan fun, creative dates! Avoid being alone together for long periods of time, especially late at night when you're tired and your guard is down. Putting yourself in this kind of situation can easily leave the door wide open for sexual compromise, and it can be dangerous.

Keep sex special for your marriage partner someday! Don't open your most precious gift until God tells you it's time—with your husband.

Here's a story for you to share with your friends at home: There was a girl (we'll call her Sue) who had a lot of pressure from her girlfriends to give in to having sex while in high school. Every day she went through the same routine during lunch: "Get with it, Sue. You're the only one who's still a virgin!" After about a month of listening to her friends' comments, Sue finally told them: "I could be like you any time I want. But you can never again be like me."

Sue was saving her gift. She knew God gave her sex to open with only one person, when she got married. In a society that accepts sex before marriage as normal, Sue chose purity, knowing that it's the unpopular, but *better*, choice. You'll have no greater gift to give your husband someday than your purity! Draw the lines *now* and hold to them!

Your "sis,"

Lisa

A Word about Sexual Pressure

God hasn't changed His mind about sex.

"Marriage should be honored by all, and the marriage bed kept pure" (Heb. 13:4). "It is God's will that you should . . . avoid sexual immorality" (1 Thess. 4:3).

The Inventor of sex has put a fence around it called marriage. Society wants to tear down the fence . . . your hormones encourage you to tear down the fence . . . and your freedom and friends at college will increase the pressure to forget the fence and "do it." If you do, you will give up the specialness of sex—and it's the specialness that makes it great.

My son has a baseball card collection. His most valuable cards are those that are either rare or in mint condition. By choosing the oftentimes unpopular road of purity, you're rare. As more and more people around you become more and more sexually active, you'll be tempted to feel that rare is weird. It's not. Rare is valuable. Keep yourself valuable and in "mint condition" for your future husband.

Remember that you are on the threshold of a new beginning. Whatever you may have done morally in high school can be put behind you now. That's what Jesus died on the cross for—to forgive our sins and to start us over with a clean slate. God says, "The blood of Jesus, his Son, purifies us from all sin" (1 John 1:7). If you turn from any past wrongs and give yourself to Christ, you can enter college's New World as a new person.

With a new beginning, you need to put some guards around the "fence." You can keep sex special if:

1. You avoid the opportunity to mess up sexually. You cannot fight sin and flirt with it at the same time. So avoid prolonged times alone with a guy . . . don't allow yourself to get to a point where you're thinking beyond the boundaries of purity . . . let your standard be known right up front to anyone you spend a lot of time with.

2. You and God draw a physical line that you will not cross. Don't wait for your first college date or some passionate emergency. You and God (He lives in your body) settle the boundary now, before the pressure hits.

3. You watch what you watch and listen to. "Guard your heart, for it is the wellspring of life" (Prov. 4:23). If you are going to save sex for marriage, don't watch or listen to input that portrays the opposite.

On Day One of college, you're starting new. Start clean, with your heart set on purity. Crown Christ Lord of your love life and your glands every day. Then you will be able to go to sleep every night—including your wedding night—with no regrets.

Ron

Budgeting Money

Dear Jessica,

As I enter my second semester, you probably think I've got college pretty well figured out by now. Well, I am "older and wiser" (stop choking, Jess), but I've learned another huge lesson recently. It's incredible . . . I come to school to study what they teach in my *classes*, but I sure wish I could get graded on everything I have to learn outside of class, too!

Anyway, basically I realized I was really unprepared to live on my own when it came to money.

You can kindly stop laughing now. At least I'm not as bad as a campus legend that tells of a freshman girl who thought she could write checks as long as she had *checks* in her checkbook, regardless of how much money she had in her account. I wasn't *that* clueless about managing money, but I did have some things to learn about balancing my checkbook (and not just on my head!).

Jessica, sit back, relax, and let me paint the scenario first semester.

Mom and Dad came with me to drop me off at school orientation week. During those first few days, we went together to a nearby bank to start my college bank account. It was pretty cool—my summer earnings, plus an allowance from Mom and Dad, gave me about $1,000 in my new account. Awesome! All I had to do was make this money last all year and I'd be set! I clearly remember one bit of instruction I received from Mom about "balancing" my first checkbook ever: "Make sure you enter the amount and number of every check you write in your checkbook, and you'll be OK." Sounds simple, right?

Somehow, I had conveniently forgotten (I still think I was never told) that the purpose of writing the amounts of checks in my checkbook was so that I could then *subtract* the money I spent and know how much money I had left in my account.

Anyway, here I was with hundreds of dollars in the bank to spend on books, college T-shirts (a definite necessity, right?), pencils, and erasers. But soon all that was paid for, and I had a lot left over—I was rich! And no one to monitor my money! College was great! I thought I could take the campus trip to Europe or Mexico and *still* have lots left over for all four years of college, but pretty soon I couldn't even get a soda from down the hall!

Where did it all go? Well, books *are* expensive, so that ate a few hundred dollars. But I've also been paying for all the leftover stuff . . . pizza, miniature golf, group outings with friends, phone bills (no, phone calls aren't free either at college like they were at home), Christmas gifts for family and friends, little surprises for this cute guy I met, and other "important" purchases!

Twenty-five pizzas and too many long-distance phone calls later (I learned to call Mom and Dad collect), suddenly I had this awful feeling that my life was spinning out of control, and pictures of debtor's prison kept floating through my mind!

In desperation, I went running to the First National Bank of Mom & Dad. "How could this be? I'm eighteen years old and filing for bankruptcy!" Where could I hide from all these terrible statements coming from the bank listing overdraft charges that I had no money to pay?

Suddenly, I was face to face with the dreaded B-word. Mom and Dad said I needed to learn how to b-u-d-g-e-t. (It *sounds* like a painful word, doesn't it?) Well, the day my life was hurtling out of control, the B-word became a friend.

I have had to learn to sit down and ask myself how much money I should spend on food, pizza (that's in a category by itself!), school supplies, clothes, fun group activities, and that cute guy. Then I know what activities I want to do and what purchases I need to make and the limit I can spend in those certain areas. And, yes—I still enter in the amount of every check I write, but now I make it over to the far right column to *subtract* what I just entered, so I know what I have in the bank. Actually, the banks invented a good system.

I also know that there are ways (just like when we'd all get together at home in high school) to have "cheap, inexpensive fun." There are games to play, places to see a movie for a dollar, small notes to send to my cute friend, and I already wrote to you about not eating too many pizzas (and therefore not tipping those delivery guys either!). Be creative (and therefore *cheap!*) with fun.

Believe me, my life is much more under control now. Of course, I don't have much money left in the bank to even budget! If you want to take up a collection for a broke freshman at college, well. . . .

Learning to like the B-word,

Lisa

A Word about Budgeting

Budget is not a four-letter word. In fact, it's a friendly word. It builds your parents' trust, gives you a financial map to keep you from getting lost, and prevents panic later on. Manage your money well, and you will have the most convincing proof of all that you are an adult.

Money maturity begins by having a clear understanding with your parents of who is paying for what. That can head off some ugly budget wars.

Now that you are managing your finances, learn to think economy. "How can I make this amount of money go the farthest?" Discover the lower prices of store brands . . . make it to the school meals you've already paid for instead of buying outside frequently . . . buy snacks in quantity at the store instead of buying them from machines . . . look for cheap, creative date ideas . . . learn to clean and repair things instead of discarding them.

And don't forget God. The biblical starting point for giving to your Lord is 10 percent. If you give to the Lord's work right off the top, you'll find that the 90 percent will go miraculously farther than 100 percent that forgets God. You say, "But money is so tight at college—I can't afford to give to God." You can't afford not to! "Bring the whole tithe into the storehouse. . . . Test me in this . . . and see if I will not throw open the floodgates of heaven and pour out so much blessing that you will not have room enough for it" (Mal. 3:10).

Ron

Take It or Leave It

Dear Jessica,

OK, OK. I know I'm famous for having the heaviest luggage around (I think my brothers started that horrible rumor!), but there *are* a lot of things girls need wherever they go. How do I know for sure that I won't really need something when I leave home—I'm better off taking *everything*, "just in case."

Remember that scene in O'Hare airport—also known as "Mount Luggage"? One of my poor brothers, after carrying all my bags, said that when *he* went to college he was just taking his toothbrush, Bible, and underwear! Well, I realized I didn't need some of the stuff I brought to school, while I had forgotten other things I really needed. I hope I can help you avoid some of the same mistakes.

Clothes. What more do I have to say about girls? We have lots of clothes and can't part with any of them! Make sure you bring clothes for each season, but *be realistic* about the clothes you'll actually need and wear. That also goes for shoes, too. You probably won't wear many high heels on campus because you usually have to walk everywhere, so bring a good pair of sneakers and flat-heeled shoes.

Don't forget a good umbrella for those rainy days, a popcorn popper for low-calorie snacks at night, an iron, at least two sets of towels and sheets (so you have a spare when you're doing laundry), at least one power strip (it seems that there is *one* outlet per room, no matter how many people live in it!), your rabbit earmuffs (if you have winters like here! *Brrrr!*), and don't forget a drying rack for some of your laundry.

During orientation week, make a trip to the local department store. You need lots of extra space to store all your stuff—a basket for cosmetics (don't forget to bring the substances that make you beautiful in the morning to put *in* the basket!), bins for under your bed, shelves for books, a shoe organizer—whatever space-savers you can find!

Also, get organized when you first get here—school gets busy real fast, so plan to make your room efficient, practical, and "aesthetically pleasing" from the very beginning. You use your room a lot—for socializing, studying, and living (not necessarily in that order). Your room is also your biggest source of identity at college, even though you share it with other human beings. Make it livable, workable, and comfortable!

Last semester, I knew a guy who had a computer he used in class to take notes with, so he got lots of information down, while I plodded along getting writer's cramp. Plus, writing papers is one of the biggest time-consumers at college—and it's a nightmare to write a paper without a computer. Fortunately, I received a personal, portable word processor for Christmas, so this semester has been much smoother, and my computer saves *lots* of time! You really can't afford *not* to bring some kind of computer or word processor.

Don't forget to raid some local stationery store or the college bookstore for all kinds of school supplies (I already mentioned those bubble-gum smelling erasers!) such as paper clips, rubber bands, and book highlighters to mark important things while reading. (NOTE: Don't use highlighters in bed when you're very tired—I still have a yellow streak down my pink comforter from when I fell asleep while studying in bed one night.) Pick up a roll of stamps at the post office, too—it'll save you hundreds of dollars each month in phone bills (unless you learn early to call home collect!). Don't forget a sturdy backpack to carry heavy books across campus in. Plus, you might want a subscription to a news magazine to keep you in touch with the real world.

Even though you'll want to bring lots of fun books to read in your "free time"—give it up now. You'll have plenty to read in college! But don't forget your Bible; that's one of the few books you'll want to bring to school. Most of all, don't forget your brain—you'll find you use that frequently. Happy packing!

Your learning-to-pack-lighter "sis,"

Lisa

A Word about Stuff

Rabbits and stuff. They both multiply fast.

You've had eighteen years to accumulate your own personal mountain of stuff—clothes you'll never wear again except on Nerd Day, old toys, books, papers, fossilized pizza crusts.

Now it's time to do yourself a favor . . . un-stuff your life! This countdown to college offers you a natural break in your life, a time to get things under control before the college-quake hits.

This is your golden opportunity to simplify your life. So clobber those closets, dive into those drawers, plunder those piles, battle those bags.

Sell what you can to help with those college bills.

Better yet, "Give to the poor" (Luke 12:33). Some of our warmest family memories are of scouring the house for stuff—good stuff—so we could take it to some homeless people. Why should we have three or six of something when others don't even have one of it?

With your life "un-stuffed," you can leave behind a home base that's sane and simplified.

It's a great feeling knowing you have what you need—and that's all. You've got an exciting marathon ahead of you. When you travel light, you can run well.

Ron

Roommate:
Living with a Stranger

Dear Jessica,

Turf is a precious thing. Jess, you play field hockey, and you know your position covers a specific area—your turf. My brother's dog, Missy, claims the spot under the kitchen hutch as "her turf." Living at home, *my* turf was one whole bedroom. I know, I know, since I was at home over fall break and Christmas, there have been rumors that my new turf is the living room couch and coffee table, where I crash for a week and recuperate from college.

Well, when you get to college you won't have much "turf." Plus, you will have all your important earthly possessions to creatively keep on *your* turf, where they won't interfere with other people's turf.

Let me reminisce with you for a moment: I remember my parents telling me about how our family moved when I was eighteen months old. Evidently I had gotten real close to our family possessions, because when I was finally reunited with our furniture six weeks later, I waddled around our new apartment and up to our chair, put my head on it, and cooed, "Love chair." I quickly made the rounds, cooing, "Love couch." "Love doll." Seventeen years later, things aren't much different at college. No wonder some girls from next door came over asking where my little sister was—they could hear her saying, "Love clothes." "Love pillow." (I never let on that I don't have a baby sister.)

During orientation week, I was the first one to move into my assigned dorm room. The next day, I came back to my room, anticipating the arrival of my new roommate—to my shock, there was not one, but *two* other girls who had moved into the room! It's hard enough to move in with *one* person you've never met before, but here we were—three strangers in a dorm room meant for two. Excuse me, here we were—three strangers and all our belongings (make-up, clothes, books, clothes, curling irons, clothes, pictures, clothes . . . you get the idea).

The task of merging the worlds of three girls and all their stuff is next to impossible. Talk about hardly any "turf"! I must have only had about 2.2 square feet to myself that whole first semester! (Since Christmas, one of the girls moved down the hall, so now we've shifted our alternate breathing plan to a regular breathing plan!)

As I lay in bed one night during the second week of school, I suddenly realized I was going to spend the next eight months sleeping three feet from two strangers. In junior high, I always wanted to have a sleepover, but now I was hoping for a night to sleep alone in a room. The concept of an eight-month sleepover was great for the first week, but the novelty quickly wore off.

One of the first differences we encountered was "lights out" time. At summer camp, it was easy because the counselors enforced "lights out" at 9:30 P.M., no exceptions. But in college, who controls the lights? I usually stayed up late, while my roommates liked lights out early—at 10:30 or 11:00 P.M.! My options? Learn Braille, flunk my classes by not studying, or gather up all my studying stuff, load it into a wheelbarrow, and move into the floor lounge after 10:30. Another disadvantage of an early lights out time was when I would get home from a date, after my roommates were asleep, and would accidentally make noise stumbling in the dark around all our possessions (I felt like a soldier navigating through a minefield). I would hear one of them turn over in bed, groan or mumble something, or—worst of all—sit up in bed to see what was going on. Coming home from a date through the "midnight minefield" almost converted me to an earlier bedtime, but I guess I loved the challenge of making it through the dark to the bathroom without tripping over the refrigerator cord!

Besides determining what time the lights went out, all three of us roommates found we had different tastes in music, clothes, and how long we each talk on the phone. Try to imagine three girls in one room with *one* phone—it's not a pretty picture.

Since we each had nowhere else to live, we had to learn how to live together. The college provided an *Official Roommate Starter Kit* to help us get to know each other. But it's really a big joke—you learn more about each other in the daily experiences of life.

Before I get writer's cramp, let me give you two C-words that can make a big difference in learning to live with a stranger (or *strangers!*).

Compromise is key! You quickly learn what ground you want to keep and the issues you can compromise on. Is it really important to blast your music at level ten, or is level four just as good, or better yet, headphones? Does your roommate prefer you to eat cookies at your desk or in her bed? Pick your battles carefully. Don't fight over everything—realize you will need to give some ground to live happily ever after.

Be *considerate.* Don't sit on the phone for two hours straight when you know your roommate is expecting a call from that cute guy. Don't drape your dirty clothes over her desk chair or shine a flashlight in her face at 2:00 A.M. Also, give your roommate some privacy. In college, all privacy is invaded because of living with other people. (Personally, when I'm sick, I'm not real thrilled about throwing up with an audience around—it's nice to have *some* privacy.) Also, remember, you can always wash your hands—I say this because you *will* need to empty the trash at *some* point in time in college—the college doesn't provide maids to do that for you.

Being considerate also means you should *respect* your roommate and her things. *Ask* to use her stereo, shampoo, or sweater—even though you live together, you're not sisters.

Keep your sense of humor! Make the best of difficult situations, and you'll find you're living with a new friend instead of a stranger.

Jess, while you're still at home—*pray* for your roommate. You don't know who she will be yet, but pray that you'll have the roommate the Lord wants you with. My mom suggested I do that, and it helped—I got some great roommates!

Hey, enjoy your turf at home for now. See you over spring break!

Your "turfless" sis,

Lisa

A Word about College Roommates

The Matchmaker has your name. Soon you'll see who you got matched up with.

The Matchmaker is your heavenly Father. The match is your roommate—if you've been praying for God to pick her. "The steps of a good man are ordered by the Lord" (Psalm 37:23, KJV), that must include a step as important as who you'll live with every day.

Pray so you can walk into that room on Day One with anticipation rather than anxiety. "Let's see what person God thought I needed to spend the next year with."

Don't be surprised if it's someone very different from you. "As iron sharpens iron, so one man sharpens another" (Prov. 27:17). God knows how much you can grow by adapting to another person's needs, tastes, idiosyncrasies, and priorities. You might say, "I already had to do that with my brother or sister." Ah yes, but at college there's no parent to arbitrate the negotiations!

If you hit some frustrations in your relationship, don't let the frustrations build up. Confront them while they're small.

Learning to love and live with a roommate is one of the best growing opportunities you have had in your life so far. By praying for your roommate—even before you know who it is—you allow God to do the choosing. By praying with your roommate through all kinds of challenges, you can tear down walls and build lifetime bonds.

I got to thinking how awesome it would be to have Jesus for a roommate. Here's what He would be like:

In humility consider others better than yourselves. Each of you should look not only to your own interests, but also to the interests of others. Your attitude should be the same as that of Christ Jesus. (Phil. 2:3–5)

If Jesus lives in you, then the person you'll live with could have a roommate like that. Let Jesus move into that dorm when you do . . . through you.

Ron

Christian College
Peer Pressure

Dear Jessica,

From your last letter it sounds like you're really making a difference for Jesus in your high school. I know it must have been hard to turn down that questionable part in the spring play, but God honors those who honor Him. Also, it's exciting to hear that one of your friends is asking more questions about knowing Jesus. It's obvious that your light is shining, and people are noticing there's something different about you.

It's tough to make a stand in high school in the midst of so much pressure, but you'll have a stronger and deeper relationship with Jesus as a result of standing firm. Let me tell you . . . the pressure doesn't stop—even at a Christian college.

What's unique about a Christian school is that there is often some "positive" pressure from friends, especially in maintaining your walk with God. Oftentimes, they are the ones who help make sure you get to church on Sunday morning, have devotions on a regular basis, and are involved in some kind of ministry. This can be really good, but even this positive pressure can turn into something negative when pushed to an extreme.

Jess, I'd like to encourage you to seek a *balanced* life here at college. It's unfortunate that some people who like to be known as "Christians who have it all together" will look down on those around them who don't. It seems they expect you to have devotions from 5:30 to 7:00 in the morning, go to the "best" church in town, and lead at least twenty off-campus ministries and ten on-campus Bible studies! (Well, maybe my example is a bit extreme, but . . .) Structure your own priorities based on what the Bible says, and learn your own limits and guidelines as to what you can be involved in. It's not worth leading that nineteenth ministry if you're falling asleep in your classes every day!

Of course the other unfortunate extreme are those who scoff at people who really are excited about serving Jesus. Not all students and even some faculty at a Christian college are deeply committed to Jesus Christ, and therefore they don't sense an urgency to pursue a life glorifying to God. Don't ever listen to or be discouraged by these sarcastic people—as long as *you* go M.A.D. ("make a difference") wherever the Lord puts you at college!

You say, "OK, well those kinds of pressure I can handle, but at least I won't have to worry about sex, alcohol, or drugs." Maybe so, but you will still face pressure to compromise. In fact, I guarantee that you will encounter a lot of pressure to participate in a lot of "gray" areas. Plus, sexual pressure and pressure to drink are growing problems on Christian college campuses. Don't expect these problems to just disappear in a Christian environment.

How can you deal with these pressures? Well, keep your eyes on Jesus, not on other people's beliefs and expectations. Know that your ultimate goal is to get to know Jesus better and learn to fall in love with him more each day. There's no such thing as being a "super" Christian, and it's destructive to be a "sarcastic, self-pleasing" Christian. Your standard should be the *Bible*. Be Christlike.

I've gotta run to my psychology class, so I'll write next time about pressures on a secular college campus. Hey, keep *making a difference* in high school—you might be the last person some of your friends could ever hear about Jesus from!

Your "sis,"

Lisa

A Word about Christian College Peer Pressure

Squeeze an egg as hard as you can—and have a lot of fun cleaning the yolk off the walls, the floor, and you. Now . . . take a hard-boiled egg and squeeze it as hard as you can. No cleanup—no splat. Two eggs, both squeezed—what's the difference? One is "squeeze-proof" because it is solid at the center.

It's important that you enter college solid at the center . . . solid because you've settled your personal convictions and won't change them. The surprise is that there is so much moral and spiritual "squeeze" at a Christian college.

On one side, you'll feel pressure from students who are "playing world," abusing their new freedom to sample sin. They really can't handle their first opportunity to make choices outside their hometown cocoon. They are trying so hard to prove they are free that they become slaves to freedom, always having to choose the opposite of Christian choices. These "slaves to freedom" will be pressuring you to "loosen up." If you're solid at the center, you'll stick to Galatians 5:13: "Do not use your freedom to indulge the sinful nature."

On the other side, you'll be squeezed by people who think there is only one narrow way to be spiritual. They're slaves too . . . slaves to formulas, externals. God's plan for His body is variety (1 Cor. 12), yet these people will insist that everyone pray, worship, serve, and believe exactly alike. Sometimes they will "play Holy Spirit," trying to help Him convict everyone of sin. Later on, folks like these divide churches over minor issues. "It is for freedom that Christ has set us free. Stand firm, then, and do not let yourselves be burdened again by a yoke of slavery" (Gal. 5:1).

There's a simple bottom line question you'll have to settle on this side of moving day: Who are you going to please? If you decide once and for all that the answer is Jesus— only Jesus—you'll never collapse . . . no matter how hard you're squeezed.

Ron

Secular College Peer Pressure

Dear Jessica,

Hey, I hope the "college freshman wisdom" I've been sharing with you the past few months is helping you, as you prepare to head to college yourself in a few months.

In your last letter you wanted to know about the pressures at a Christian school and at a secular university. Here's "Pressures, Part Two," answering your questions about secular schools.

Since I chose to attend a Christian school, I haven't experienced firsthand some of the pressures at a secular school, but I've had many friends who chose that option for college. Frankly, I've heard little *positive* feedback from Christian friends about a secular university.

My friends have shared with me that, first of all, there is a pervasive "anti-Christian" atmosphere on a secular campus. Faculty, administration, and friends have little tolerance or sympathy for Christianity or the Bible. One friend has told me that at his secular university there is actually more attention and tolerance for other religious beliefs, the views of homosexuals, and those in religious cults than there is for Christians.

On the first day of class, one Christian student heard his professor say: "I know there are a few of you in here who will choose to use assignments to communicate your beliefs. If you do not give me the evolutionistic answer in your assignments, I will fail you. If you can't do that, then drop my class today." A hard choice for a Christian—do you fail? Do you drop the class? Do you witness to the professor?

The only sacred thing on the secular college campus today is *each individual's right* to believe something, without pushing it off on someone else. *Tolerance* is the reigning philosophy. A friend told me he feels the unspoken attitude from his peers on a secular campus is: "Oh, you're a Christian, that's great. Just keep it to yourself. I'm an alcoholic. Don't try to change me. Don't make me uncomfortable. Just don't interfere with my comfort zone." He mentioned how he can easily talk about God with his non-Christian friends, but as soon as he mentions "Jesus," he immediately knows that he has crossed over the unspoken "comfort line." God is a safe topic to have a theological discussion about, but although friends will tolerate hearing Jesus mentioned, they become silent and look away, which presents one of the worst social pressures for a Christian student.

Along with this unsympathetic attitude toward Christianity on secular campuses, there is little (or no) concept of morality among students. Sex and drinking are rarely hidden, because almost everybody *is* doing it. Actually, a fellow freshman friend of mine at a secular school found 75 percent of the guys on his floor were having sex on Friday Night. (Often guys leave a necktie on their doorknob when their girlfriend is inside, so others won't disturb them.

It is assumed that everybody at a secular school drinks alcohol. On many campuses, it's the norm for students to go to a local bar after a final exam, and sometimes professors will even treat upperclassmen to a few drinks. College students are big business for bars, even from students who are underage, since it's not too difficult to get a fake ID.

I learned of one Christian guy who went to school this year and had decided not to drink. One month later he came back to his dorm room drunk. Why? Erosion. He wore down. He got into a group that offered him companionship and filled his desperate need for identity. To these friends, he wasn't just one in forty thousand in the college administrative office computer—he was an *individual* with his drinking friends, cared for in the middle of the masses.

Unfortunately, after giving in to sexual or drinking pressures, it's the once-committed *Christian* students who try to drag down other Christian friends. "Misery loves company," and so does a guilty conscience. One of the worst traps at college is when Christian friends begin to drag you down into things they've fallen into.

Why are these problems found everywhere on a secular campus? We *all* have an "emotional support tank" that needs continual filling. If a person doesn't depend on a personal relationship with Jesus Christ to fill that emotional support tank, pretty soon they'll turn and seek other things to meet that longing for companionship. This need for companionship started long ago in the Garden of Eden when Adam needed Eve. That same need is found on every secular college campus today—the need to "belong" and be an individual, in the midst of 39,999 other people! That's why fraternities, sororities, drinking parties, and sexual relationships are everywhere—it's people striving to find intimacy and companionship.

If you do decide to attend a secular college campus, make sure you immediately plug into some strong "support base" like InterVarsity, a Bible study group, a church you like, or even Christian housing. You need to have a group of people you meet with *regularly* who are a support for you and who share your beliefs and priorities.

Right now, while you're still in high school, cultivate your relationship with Jesus. Be strong when you get to a secular school and make your stance known—if people know what you stand for, it's easier to hold your ground, they know you won't budge. It's a lonely road to choose, but Jesus took the loneliest road for *you*.

I know this is a lot of information to take in at once, but I hope some of these experiences can help answer any questions you or your friends have. Ultimately, stay close to Jesus; use *him* as your measuring stick, not other Christians or people around you!

Your "sis,"

Lisa

A Word about Secular College Peer Pressure

If you tried to play football or soccer on a field with no boundaries, you wouldn't have a game.

Most people at secular colleges are playing life as if there were no boundaries. The result is chaos. Because you belong to Jesus Christ, you need to know where your boundaries are. There won't be any around you, so you'll have to bring them inside you.

When you're God's ambassador to a secular school, you need the "Conqueror's Survival Kit." It has five tools in it:

1. A Firsthand Faith. Your parents' or your church's faith won't survive the pressure. Be sure you have an active, growing, personal relationship with Jesus. If your faith depends on your environment, "Good-bye, Jesus."

2. A Consistent Stand. The best way to reduce peer pressure is to take the same stand every time. Once people see there is only one you, they will usually lay off and let you be that person.

3. A "No Compromise" Morality. Satan usually destroys a Christian by erosion, not explosion. He will try to wear you down to sins you never thought you would commit just by getting you to make a series of little compromises. Say no to the first compromise; it's the easiest one to resist.

4. A Support Team. Peer pressure is your friend if the group is going God's way. Go wherever you have to go to find a group of believers your age who share your convictions.

5. A "Make a Difference" Attitude. God sends you to a college to change your environment, not just to survive. If your goal is just to survive, you won't. When you're actively fighting for people's lives, you know compromise is too costly.

There's a challenging Christian song that asks, "Will you be the one to stand when those around you fall? Will you be the one to take His light into a darkened world?" Say to Him today, "I will be the one!"

Ron

Long-Distance Romance

Dear Jessica,

How's your "sweetheart" doing? It sounds like you two had a fun Valentine's Day last week. Actually, that day of romance made me think about couples that are here at college. One kind of couple rarely stays together long.

No, this kind of couple isn't some mismatched odd couple—you know, the quiet, behind-the-scenes math major guy dating the outspoken, up-front communications major girl. This couple is made up of two people who live miles and hours apart. It's the sad saga of long-distance romance.

Most people agree that one of the dumbest things in the world is coming to college "committed." When you live miles apart from your boyfriend, you're not just apart physically, but you quickly become distant emotionally, mentally, and even spiritually! Most long-distance romances break up simply because two people find themselves living in two totally different worlds—he's developing in one environment, while you're growing in a completely different setting!

I wish I had an exact percentage for you, but the pattern of all my fellow freshmen girlfriends who came to college "committed" was this: They looked forward to fall break to spend time with their boyfriends at home, but by Christmas almost every one of them had broken up with their boyfriends back home—including myself!

To help avoid unnecessary pain, a smart thing to do is to "renegotiate" your relationship with your boyfriend *before* you come to college. To think that you both won't want to date anybody else may be shortsighted. To say you're only dating one guy back home before even meeting any other guy at college is like saying you love generic cereal, and then turning the corner in the grocery store to find an aisle full of colorful fun cereals! You never *knew* before that Apple Jacks and Fruit Loops even existed!

When you come to college committed, realize that most of your budget will probably go toward huge phone bills (unless your boyfriend's parents really don't mind you calling him collect from halfway across the country every night). Also, because you're "committed," you limit your social involvement because you spend more time on the phone than getting to know new people, plus you don't go out as often with friends. I've been told that in most cases the friends you make in college are your friends for life. That doesn't mean you forget all your friends from high school. But what it does mean is that you should invest in developing relationships at college, especially early on in your freshman year. Wherever you are, make sure to be all there! *Live* life to the fullest in college, and get to know all kinds of people!

Now don't run out and break up with your boyfriend right after he spent all that money on you for Valentine's Day— enjoy dating right now (and who knows, your relationship could be one of the few to stand the test of being miles apart!). But be realistic. Understand that you will meet lots of new guys at college, plus some you'll want to know better!

For high school sweethearts, it helps to know *now* that trying to keep the sweetness in your relationship during college could end up being a bitter experience!

Your long-distance-relationship-warning "sis,"

Lisa

A Word about Long-Distance Romance

Long-distance phone calls cost a lot. So do long-distance romances.

In fact, they usually cost someone a broken heart. Why do people go to college committed to someone back home? Obviously, it's because of some deep feelings—probably the closest feelings to real love they have ever felt.

But there's a painful miscalculation in going to the New World with a "Taken" sign on. You're underestimating how much and how fast you will change there. In only a few months, you will not be the same person who left for college. The person you left will either change in that period of time or stay the same because they stayed in the Old World. In either case, a gap will develop. And it will hurt.

Locking yourself up in a steady relationship "back there" sets you up for all kinds of emotional struggle—guilt over other attractions, frustration over communication problems, confusion over mixed feelings, "schizo-ness" from trying to live in two different worlds.

Because your steady and the Old World is all you can see, you'll be reluctant to renegotiate an open relationship. But listen to the voices who have seen the New World, who know what's there. They will almost unanimously say, "Come with your options open." If what you have at home is real, it will stand the test. If God has someone else for you in the New World, you'll avoid breaking one—and maybe two—hearts.

Ron

Extracurricular Buffet

Dear Jessica,

Have you and your friends hit the cruise control button yet at this point in your senior year? Springtime senior year is probably the most frustrating time for any high school teacher—it seems that most seniors have turned off their brains. Well, enjoy your "cruising" time because there won't be much of that in college!

Congratulations about that scholarship you've been nominated for! I'm sure all your extra involvement at school has really helped. I remember those wonderful high school days of having some *extra* time to be able to do those fun *extra*curricular activities. It's a little different in college.

Spring of my junior year in high school, I received a phone call from the college I really hoped to attend. It was a college senior who worked in the school's admissions office. He just wanted to ask me some questions and share some of his college experiences with me. He was interested in which subject I wanted to major in and which activities I hoped to be a part of in college.

Well, I shared with this guy the activities I was currently involved with in high school: president of the school service organization, president of the choir, feature editor for the school newspaper, computer editor for the school yearbook, Honor Society, the school peer counseling program, the school band, and a student leader in the Campus Life club ministry. Plus, I had various other commitments throughout the school year for different projects. I *loved* being involved in high school!

Then . . . my naivete showed through. I'm sure I really gave this guy the best laugh of his college career that night right there on the phone. I told him: "I'd like to have three majors—Communications, Bible, and French. Then I'd like two minors—Christian Education and Psychology. Plus, of course, I want to stay real involved in lots of activities—various ministries, singing, writing for the newspaper and yearbook, etc."

He laughed and simply said, "Well, just wait until you get here." He was right. I didn't understand his comment until I got here. Now *I* even laugh at all those far-fetched goals I had for college!

Actually, when I got to college during orientation week they had booths and booths representing various activities and ministries on and off campus. After this barrage of information, I came back to my room with brochures and flyers about *everything* the college had to offer. I was thrilled that they had so many great activities to join! Meanwhile, I still had to think practically about starting a bank account; I still wanted three majors; I considered running for president of my class during orientation week; I was meeting new people constantly; I wanted to join every great activity on campus . . . obviously, orientation week is the most unrealistic week of your entire life. I had encountered *opportunity overload!* How could I possibly sort out what to do and what not to do? I think I actually considered going out for everything but the football team.

After a "reality check" with my parents, I realized I needed to go easy deciding what responsibilities I took on in this new world of college. I quickly learned that high school and college are very different. For example, college studies are much more time-consuming than high school homework.

I decided it was probably best to hold off joining any activities until I knew if I could juggle studying, social times, and other jobs only I could do (like laundry and brushing my teeth). Actually, the first activity I became involved with was a youth ministry to junior high school kids. I began to help out in this Junior Varsity Campus Life club just a few weeks into fall semester, but I had waited long enough that I had begun to establish a routine in my new environment. Eventually, I even had time to have a sleepover in the dorm with sixteen junior high girls—talk about absolute chaos (and fun)! Their ultimate dream of being away from their parents for a night with all their friends quickly turned into a very sleepless night for me!

I suggest that when you get here, you *do* get involved in *some* activities that appeal to you, but *don't* get involved in too much too soon. Why? It's crazy! You have to make sure you have enough time to study, time for the Lord, time for a ministry, time for church, time to sleep, and time to stay sane. Then enter college life gradually. I think that's one of the smart things I did here at college—I've been entering activities and ministries *gradually*. I mentioned that last semester I started helping in the junior high ministry. This semester I became the lead singer in a contemporary Christian band, where we hope to sing at youth events, juvenile detention centers, and some campus events. And recently I was accepted into the women's singing group on campus for sophomore year. That will add more responsibility to my schedule, and it also involves some travel times away from classes and away from my family because I can't go home on some breaks. This year, that activity would have created extra stress and made managing my time a miserable experience. Every activity wants you to be involved in it, but *you* must decide. To avoid over-load at college, add activities *gradually.*

Be careful to avoid the other extreme of *wasting* your time. I've seen some of my friends squander their time on watching too much TV or hanging out in the lounge for hours at a time. It's unfortunate. They could be gaining much more from their college experience.

I hope some of this will help make your decisions easier. There's a lot to know, and learning the best way to manage your time isn't something you learn in classes. I didn't have an older brother or sister to share helpful hints with me, so I hope some of my experiences can help *you* when you get to college.

By the way, no, I'm not taking three majors. One is fine for now. And I've forgotten about having two minors—there's not time! But if I *do* become more ambitious to *try*—I'll quickly call that guy from admissions and tell him I did it!

Tell everyone at home "hi" !

Living in reality,

Lisa

A Word about the Extracurricular Buffet

extra \ 'ek-stre \ adj.: beyond what is usual or necessary

If all that senior year mail from 628 colleges made you feel wanted, wait until orientation week at college. You'll be pursued by choirs, clubs, publications, organizations—the "Body Snatchers" trying to sign you up for their "extra."

You may be tempted to sign up for six or seven of them. Don't. Learning to manage major-league studying and your own life will take more of you than you think.

So keep the main thing the main thing—your studies! A lot of college freshmen make a major mistake—overcommitment. If you add more than one or two "extras," you may meet the ugliest "pro" on campus . . . pro-bation. That's the academic "do or die" pressure you feel all through second semester because your grade point didn't make it first semester.

Now it isn't that you should live in the library for four years. Just be selective in choosing an extracurricular activity—one from which you can profit and grow the most. Then, as your college career goes on, you can add or substitute other activities. It's not good to be Jen One-Dimension. The right balance helps you become a well-rounded person (so does college food!).

And don't get so tied up in on-campus extras that you don't have time for an off-campus mission for Jesus. Balance also means getting out of the college cocoon and carrying the light to the world.

You have a great four-year race ahead of you . . . and a good run depends on a good start. Don't try to carry too much with you on your first lap.

Ron

Dating at College

Dear Jessica,

It sounds like you had a great time with your family in Florida over spring break! Our spring break is coming up in a couple weeks. I can't wait to get some time off from school, but I will miss my new friends—especially a particular guy I've met. His name's Rick and he's really nice.

OK, yes, I'd like to write about one of the most favorite (or unfavorite, depending on your perspective) topics of most red-blooded females—DATING!

You wanted to know in your last letter what dating was like at college. First of all, you've never seen so many guys and girls checking each other out as during the first week of college! It's as if guys had never seen normal girls before (or maybe they were just staring because we had chocolate milk mustaches on our mouths!), and it's like girls had never seen normal guys before! Basically, it's a whole new world of people to get to know.

A couple thoughts. Even though you'll meet lots of great guys, don't rush into dating any one person steadily. Take some good time to really get to know each other as *good friends*. In college, you'll see lots of different dimensions to people— what they believe, what foods they like, what hobbies and activities they enjoy, what they really look like in the middle of the night during a fire drill, and much more! Don't rush relationships—some guys get nervous thinking that girls are just out looking for a husband, so take your time. (and don't let guys rush *you* either!) Enjoy being study partners or being involved in a ministry or school activity together. Spend time getting to know each other!

Here's some wise advice I was once told: "Never steadily date someone you wouldn't consider committing the rest of your life to." In college, start thinking about *long-term* questions like: How does this guy treat his family? How does he treat me? How is his walk with the Lord? Much of high school dating focuses on the superficial qualities in each other: How do I look together with him? Are we a cute couple? Obviously, a committed, long-term relationship has to be built on more than shallowness.

At college, you don't always have to wait for a guy to ask you out. Yes, I'm traditional, and I like the guy to do the initial asking. But when you go out in groups, feel free to get big groups of girls *and* guys together—it's a nice time to get to know each other casually. Also, on most college campuses, they have a special day or weekend for the girls to ask out the guys for a fun date. At my school, they call this T.W.I.R.P. weekend. T.W.I.R.P. stands for "The Women Initiate Romantic Pursuits" (or "The Woman Is Required to Pay"!). Some guys love this idea, because it sure takes the pressure off them! Have fun with this opportunity if it comes your way. And hey, if your college doesn't have a day like this, plan one with your friends and spread it around campus! I'm sure some guys will love it. Be friends and plan a fun, creative date.

An idea: Most guys have always had a mother around to pamper them and do special things for them. At college, there usually isn't someone to give special little treats to these "motherless" guys. As the old saying goes, "The way to a man's heart is through his stomach." I believe this, since I've seen guys enthusiastically munch on chocolate chip cookies baked "just for them." Surprise a guy or that "special someone" with some specially baked cookies, his favorite candy bar, an encouraging note, a care package waiting for him in the post office, or whatever. Be creative! How can a guy argue with a woman who showers him with yummy gifts?

Some tips about romance at college: Don't have high expectations—all guys have to get up the nerve to ask a girl out for a date. There will be many opportunities for *you* to ask that special guy out for a banquet or concert. Also, dress and act like you want to be treated by a guy—I've noticed most guys like a girl who *enjoys* being feminine. Be good friends with guys, because not every relationship has to be romantic. You can *be a friend* (and sister!) in creative ways.

Practice baking chocolate chip cookies while you're at home—it's not as easy as Mom makes it look!

See you over spring break!

Enjoying being friends with guys,

Lisa

A Word about Going Steady

According to ancient Indian tradition, when you die you go to the Happy Hunting Ground. Arriving on your college campus, you may think you've reached the Happy Hunting Ground without dying . . . at least if it's the opposite sex you're hunting.

But put your bow and arrow down. You'll miss a lot of relationships if you get swept into the Great Date Chase.

Superficiality was for high school. College is your chance for real-lationships. The key is to focus on building friendships with the opposite sex, not romances. You make friends . . . let God make one of them into a romance.

When friendship is your agenda, a relationship can develop without the cat-and-mouse tension of romantic pursuit. Unlike date-chasing, friend-building . . .

- Focuses on making the other person feel important instead of trying to impress him. You can relax and be yourself.
- Isn't charged with the pressure of a physical agenda—"How far are we going to go tonight?" With the sexual thing a non-issue, you can really get to know each other as people.
- Can involve a group instead of a couple. Again, you can relax and be yourself more easily if you aren't in the pressure situation of trying to carry the evening by yourself.
- Helps a guy build up the confidence he needs for a deeper relationship without risking romantic rejection.
- Keeps a woman from the loneliness that results from not being asked out. Since friend activities are not the big deal a date is, there will be a lot more socially active nights.
- Gives you a chance to become the kind of person you want to marry someday.

Graduation from high school can mean graduation from the frustration and immaturity of the Great Date Chase, and graduation into the better idea of friendship-building.

And you won't lose on romance either. Instead, you'll open the door to falling in love with a lifetime best friend.

Jon

Staying in Touch with God

Dear Jessica,

How are things going at school? Did you get that bear of a term paper done yet? Well, I've been working on lots of "bears" of papers lately! Since spring break, keeping my mind on anything indoors—instead of the sunny outdoors—has been a losing battle! Everyone has spring fever around here since the weather has gotten warmer. I'm sure your teachers have given up instilling any new information in your minds now that graduation is only a couple of months away.

Well, even though the sunshine has taken my attention away from some other priorities, I've had some really special times with Jesus lately. It's been neat to go and sit outdoors to read the Bible and pray.

It hasn't always been easy to be consistent, but I've really been working on keeping a regular time with the Lord each day. My relationship with Jesus is the most important one in my life, and I need to make sure it gets top priority in my day.

I've read my Bible throughout the school year, but, unfortunately, sometimes it's been at the very end of my day, when I'm absolutely exhausted, and have history facts and math formulas running through my head! Actually, a few times I've fallen asleep at night while reading my Bible, and then I wake up to find my Bible crushed between the mattress and the wall. Great devotions, huh?

My relationship with Jesus should be like every other relationship I have (except it's the highest priority!). It should be like the one I have with this guy I've dated a few times; I look forward to telling Rick about exciting events in my day, my hopes for the future, and even about problems with classes or friends. Sharing some "talking time" with him is one of the high points in my day.

Spending time with Jesus needs to be the highest point in my day, and the one priority that never changes in my schedule. He's always waiting to hear from me about what's going on in my life. Plus, His Word has so much for me to learn *now*, while I'm in college. Of course the Bible will still be around after I graduate from college—but what if Jesus comes back tomorrow? Will I know him better tomorrow because of time I spent with Him today and many yesterdays?

Time for God needs to be the one non-negotiable in your life at college. Let everything else get a lower priority—but not your time with Jesus. He wants to share all of your excitements and heartaches. I know some people who spend their time with God in the morning and then carry what they learned throughout the day with them. Others have a quiet time with Jesus at night and reread the passage the next morning. One girl makes sure she reads her Bible every day after lunch. Just pick a time and stick to it! This is between you and God—your parents, professors, and friends have nothing to do with it!

At a secular university, it'll be hard to keep your time with God in the midst of friends who don't share that priority with you. And at a Christian school, it's easy to feel like you're spending lots of time with God in your classes, chapel, and studies—but spend *personal* time with Jesus. Plus, on Sundays, don't attend Bedside Baptist Church (otherwise known as "sleeping in"). Make sure you get up on time to get to church—keep it a priority!

Remember the quote: "Does God seem far away? If so, guess who moved?" Stay close to Jesus—He loved us enough to die for us. Make sure you spend quality time (when you're awake!) getting to know Him better and learning to love Him more. College is a time when you're making life-changing decisions in the midst of many different voices (friends, parents, professors). Make sure you know where *Jesus* is leading you!

Your time for God can easily get crowded out of your busy life at college—guard that time, and keep it for Him! And if you haven't already, start a regular time with Jesus *now*, during your last few weeks of high school. It's easier to make that important time a part of your daily routine sooner than later!

Your "sis,"

Lisa

A Word about Staying in Touch with God

They called it "The Rotor." It was a popular ride at the amusement park I loved to go to as a kid. "The Rotor" was like a giant washing machine tub—it was round and it rotated, faster and faster. Once it started spinning, the floor underneath you dropped away—the screams must have broken every window in the neighborhood. People were left suspended on a tiny ledge, flattened against the wall by centrifugal force.

Centrifugal force is what can destroy your closeness with God in college. Your life will be spinning faster there than it ever has before. Without you even knowing it, Jesus can be spun right to the outer edge of your life. And you will find yourself far from your Lord just when you need Him more than ever.

It doesn't have to be that way. Set a time each day that is Jesus' time and that no one else can have. Period. You may need to make your Jesus-time different for different days of the week because of your class schedule . . . but when it's Tuesday, put a "reserved for Jesus" sign on your regular Tuesday Jesus-time. Whenever possible, start your day with the Lord—He's a lot less likely to get squeezed out than later in the day, and you're a lot more likely to handle your day victoriously.

When your life is books, the Bible can become just another book. It's not. The Bible is God's love letter to you and your personal link to Jesus' love and leading. So when you pick up your Bible, picture Jesus in your room with you, speaking to you the words you're reading. And listen for an application you can make that day—a specific obedience, spawned by something He said.

Jesus teaches us to "seek first His kingdom and His righteousness, and all these things will be given to you as well" (Matt. 6:33). He will have a lot of competition for "first" when the college rotor starts speeding up. Don't let anyone or anything else have His time. No one else loved you enough to die for you.

Ron

Professors Are People Too

Dear Jessica,

In high school, I know there is usually a lot of distance between teachers and students. In college, there's still distance, but, incredibly, you'll find that professors are actually *people* too! Yes, they have families and feelings, and they even have fun.

At a secular university it's often harder to get to know professors because their classes are so large. Sometimes the professor isn't even the one who will grade your papers; it may be his teaching assistant. However, one advantage of attending a private school with an attendance of a couple thousand is that you have the opportunity to get to know some of the professors in a more personal way.

It's been nice this first year of school because most teachers understand that, for a freshman, life really can be a circus, trying to juggle studies, friends, laundry, etc. But at some larger schools where the ratio is one teacher per 4 million students, you might get lost in the cracks.

Also, as you begin to get interested in a particular area of study or major—you'll find some professors who are very willing to sit down and have lunch with you and share their own experiences. There is *so much* to be gained and learned by spending time with professors!

Another important fact about professors is that they are all different people with different personalities. The first couple weeks of school, while you're learning to study your syllabus and books, spend some time *studying* your professors! Learn about each professor's style, personality, expectations, assignments, and quirks. Taking time to study your professors can really help as you study for their tests, write papers, and communicate with them outside of class.

Don't let all the activity and priorities at college rob you of some valuable time you could spend getting to know your professors. Take time to meet a new friend . . . I hear sometimes they'll even be your friend *after* you graduate from college!

Your "sis,"

Lisa

A Word about Professors

It's 8:00 A.M. on a Monday morning in August—your first class in college. In your hand is a new, untested Bic pen . . . on your desk is an untouched notebook and a twenty-five pound textbook . . . and in front of you is the Giver of Grades, the Keeper of the Academic Keys—your professor.

Prepare to get to know this person. Knowing your subject will not be enough . . . you will need to know what this professor expects, emphasizes, and examines. Some profs you will take to, others will turn you off. But don't let that change your commitment to know your professor. "Professorology" involves:

1. Displaying interest in the subject. You may not care much about his or her subject, but your professor

probably cares a lot about it. Whether or not the subject lights your fire, take good notes, ask good questions, make good comments.

2. Asking for help. When you're struggling, ask for help . . . immediately.

3. Showing respect. "Submit yourselves for the Lord's sake to every authority" (1 Pet. 2:13). Be friendly, say thank you, and ask about the things that seem to be important to your professor.

Every once in a while, you may find a professor you just can't handle. Remember those helpful letters TTSP—"This Too Shall Pass."

"Good morning, class."

Oops—your first class has begun.

"This is Psychology 101."

Well, yeah . . . but you know it's more than that. It's Professorology 101!

Ron

Friendships

Dear Jessica,

    With all the pressure that college involves, taking time out with friends is a blast! A bunch of us just came back from the local downtown area where we walked a couple blocks to a Dairy Queen. What a great Friday night with a group of friends!

    Jess, you'll see the difference between high school friends and college friends. In high school, you *mostly* see friends at school, the library, the mall, the movies, church. In college, however, you see your friends *all* the time (in fact, you live with them around the clock!) if you live on campus. You know how you cover up your pimples each morning with make-up? Well, when you get here, the people you live with will know you have pimples because they'll see them *before* you cover them up! One of my roommates wears curlers at night while she sleeps—I bet most of her high school friends never saw her like that!

    We girls know that there is much preparation that goes into looking good before we ever step outside the door and enter the world each day. Most friends at school or on a date never saw the "before" picture of you in the morning. They got the nice, retouched "after" picture. Even on high school retreats no one saw you look real bad because you can cover up most faults for three days.

    It's hard to hide love-handles, your green complexion scrub, and your bubble-gum smelling toothpaste for long when you *live* with friends. But you know what? You quickly learn that the people who see you stumble out of bed with morning breath and matted hair and *still* want to hang out with you will be your true friends.

Physical imperfections aren't the only flaws your new friends will see. They see when you're hurt and crying, when you're excited about a date, or when you break up with your boyfriend from home. You share a lot of life together, and this draws you closer to each other.

It definitely takes a sense of humor and a willingness to be vulnerable around your new live-in neighbors. But life is so much richer and exciting when it's shared with those around you!

About making friends here at school: Take full advantage of the first couple weeks of college to get to know everyone. There's a brief window of opportunity—just a few weeks—to comfortably meet people. After that point, it begins to be difficult to introduce yourself to people. It's a mistake to not use that "one-time window" to get to know people. As I look back over this past year even, the people I've been closest to are the ones I met during those first few weeks.

During those first couple of weeks you also have the opportunity to create your identity for college. You can choose to be any person you want at college. It's one of those rare moments in life when you have a fresh start, a blank piece of paper, when no one knows who you are. But be genuine. I see masks that people put on and experiment with—they try new clothing styles, new hairstyles, new ways of talking. Quickly carve out your identity, and make a stand on what you believe. Decide which way those around you seem to be heading, and make sure it's the direction you want to go. Remember, the friends you pick determine the course of college and, most likely, the rest of your life.

College is full of lots of new people to get to know and spend time with, but be careful. As my wise parents shared with me in high school, "Tell me your friends, and I'll tell you your future."

Your "sis" and *friend*,

Lisa

A Word about Friendships

When I'm at the airport to fly to Chicago, I find that there are a lot of nice planes there. Some are bigger than the one I'm ticketed for; others are newer or leaving sooner. But that doesn't matter. I need to pick the one that's going where I want to end up.

It's that way with college friends. Unlike high school friends, college friends tend to be yours for life. And even if you never see them again, their influence will mark you for life. Because you're away from home, your college friends virtually become your family.

So choose them well. Make sure they're going where you want to end up—in your values, your character, your relationship with God.

And don't ruin the beauty of friendship by letting your friends take over your life. If you do, you'll soon be so far behind that you'll be left with two lousy choices: Forget your friends to survive academically, or die academically—in which case you won't even be where your friends are!

A lot of people love to sing that lyric, "Friends are friends forever when the Lord's the Lord of them." In college, you can do more than sing the song—you can live it!

Ron

Gray Areas

Dear Jessica,

Graduation is getting closer and closer. I can hear strains of the high school band playing "Pomp and Circumstance" and see you receive your diploma. . . . Oh, the excitement of it all! I'll be home in time to be at graduation—I'm happy for you!

Before I get carried away with anticipation, here are some things I've learned about colors.

Black and white are easy to distinguish from one another. It would be nice if all adult issues in life were either black or white, right or wrong. Unfortunately, a lot of issues actually fall into an in-between middle—a "gray" zone. In high school, your parents and teachers decide the outcome of many gray areas for you. In college, *you* are the one who often makes the final decision about these gray issues.

As a Christian student at either a secular or Christian college, you need to make some decisions about *standing firm* for Jesus at either school. In either environment, trying to deal with gray areas can eventually erode so much away that you end up compromising in some way.

For example, how will you handle the pressure to drink? How will you handle it if you're underage and a few of the girls on your floor invite you to get a fake ID card to get you into bars? It might happen.

What kinds of movies are you going to watch? Movies are a big part of college entertainment on any campus you attend. There's little discretion among college students when it comes to being discerning about what movies they should and shouldn't see. What will be the distinguishing factor between what morality *you* will endorse and the morality (or *no* morality!) your peers endorse?

With the heavy pressure to get good grades, will you resort to cheating and plagiarism? "Of course not!" you say. Well, what about when you have a major paper due in twenty-four hours, plus two major exams, and a friend offers you a paper to use that she wrote on the same topic?

When it comes to sexual pressure, what boundaries will you draw? What physical intimacies do you want to *save* for your marriage partner? Decide now, and don't compromise!

A brief word about college rules. When a student signs any commitment saying she (or he) will not be involved in certain activities while enrolled at that particular school, there is an obligation on behalf of the student to fulfill that commitment. Be a person of *integrity*—if you sign something and agree to it, then live and abide by it. Otherwise, simply choose another school. This world doesn't need any more people who back out of commitments—it's not to be respected, and, actually, it's not real original either. What the Lord and this world *do* need are people of integrity, people who live by commitments they make.

There are other gray areas—but these are some of the biggest ones. Decide *now*. Once you decide what direction you're headed and what stance you're making, it makes life a lot easier than casually choosing to make crucial life decisions along the way. Don't wait until you get into gray, pressure-filled situations. Choose now who you'll be and who you'll serve.

Don't let Jesus down. He loves us so much He died for us—so we could spend eternity with Him in heaven. Is it really worth playing in gray areas that satisfy and make us accepted for such a short time?

Learning to stand firm,

Lisa

A Word about Gray Areas

Frogs are not very smart.

Now if you throw a frog into a pot of boiling water, it will immediately say to itself, "I am going to die." So even a frog is smart enough to jump out of a hot pot.

But if you put that same frog in a pot of warm water (I can't think of any reason why you would), it will say, "I am going to swim." If the heat is turned up gradually, it won't even notice. And it will die in that same pot of water it jumped from before. One word made the difference between life and death for the frog: gradual.

A lot of great people have "died" morally in the same way, especially in college. With so many people around you going crazy with their new freedom, it's hard not to change for the worse yourself. Oh, not suddenly; the devil knows you probably wouldn't go along if he walked up to you and said, "Hi, I'm the devil. Come with me and let me ruin your life." So he'll try the approach that has worked so well on others—gradual compromises. One day you wake up saying, "How did I get here? I was sure I would never do what I've done . . . give up what I've given up . . . feel this way."

If the destroyer of futures cannot get you to do what's obviously wrong, he'll settle right now for what's merely questionable. Then after he has worn down your resistance and made you feel comfortable with the questionable, he will give you an opportunity to do more. His plan to bring you down follows this inevitable sequence: "After desire has conceived, it gives birth to sin; and sin, when it is full-grown, gives birth to death" (James 1:15).

The easiest compromise to fight is the first compromise, the temptation to dabble in a little gray. Your best defense against "the invasion of the gray monster" is:

> 1. *Decide in advance—before you hit college—where your lines are. That includes everything from what you will and will not watch and where you will and will not go, to who you will and will not date.*
> 2. *Make your standards a promise to God. That makes it real binding. Write down your promises to God so you can often review and pray over them.*
> 3. *Say no to the first temptation.*

If you want no regrets and God's best, learn to see another color when you see gray—red, for stop.

Ron

It All Comes Down to This

Dear Jessica,

Wow! What a year it's been for both of us! I've almost survived my freshman year of college, and you actually finished your senior term paper just in time for high school graduation! (Just kidding.)

Well, I know you've had a lot of questions this past year about college, and I've tried to share with you some important things I've been learning. Even though we've talked about a million little things for college, the most important thing to remember is to keep your eyes on Jesus. He's got the whole plan of your life in front of him, and he knows you best! Don't forget to *TRUST JESUS* all the way. Give *everything* to him—dating, studying, future plans, relationships. I have a great (and *true!*) quote over my desk at school: "God always gives His best to those who leave the choice to Him."

I've gotta share a great Bible verse that someone shared with me before I left for college: "'For I know the plans I have for you,' declares the Lord, 'plans for good and not for evil, to give you a future and a hope'" (Jer. 29:11, TLB). That verse has carried me through my first year of college, and I believe it'll carry me through my sophomore year and all the years ahead!

Know that there will be some tough times ahead as you adjust to the pleasures and pressures of college life. But remember who holds the blueprint for your life. Don't fall into comparing yourself with those around you—keep Jesus as your standard and your guideline. He's the only One who will give you strength to get you through every situation this next year as a freshman.

Don't shove Jesus out of the picture as you get busy at college. Make Him the center of your life and day, and remember that "in all things God works for the good of those who love Him" (rom. 8:28). He won't leave you hanging!

Happy studying for final exams and happy packing for college! I'll be home next week to see you at high school graduation and to congratulate you on being a *freshman!*

Your faithful friend and almost a sophomore,

Lisa

A Word about What It Comes Down To

We've done our best to prepare you for the new world ahead. But no matter how much information you have, there's still a lot of "unknown" out there, right?

Well, that's OK, because now you have a wonderful chance to hang on to your Savior and see all that He can mean.

I remember driving into the mountains one night in a blinding blizzard. Hardly anyone was on the road . . . I wouldn't have been if I weren't speaking for a retreat in the mountains. The road was disappearing rapidly under heavy snow, and I could barely see beyond the hood of my car.

I got to my destination OK because of a snowplow. I got behind a big old snowplow and stayed close all the way. I couldn't see the road, but he could. And he was always just ahead of me, clearing the way.

That's what Jesus said He would do for you in one of His most excellent promises. I learned it in college, and I've claimed it over and over again when the road ahead was uncertain. Jesus said, "When He [the Good Shepherd] has brought out all His own, He goes on ahead of them" (John 10:4).

Everywhere you are about to go, Jesus your Shepherd will go there ahead of you and clear the way. He's already in your New World of college, getting your spot ready, your future friends ready, your needs cared for.

So everywhere you walk in your world of new beginnings, you will find your Shepherd's footprint.

That's all you need to know.

Ron

Postscript

Long before our daughter Lisa had her first day of college, she baked her first cake. Actually, she was only five years old when she announced to her mom and me, "I'm baking a cake for you —I'm doing it all by myself."

I could hear a lot of bustle and banging in the kitchen . . . then the aroma of something baking. I was reading in the living room when a sad-faced little girl entered, carrying her creation in front of her. "Here it is, Daddy," Lisa said with obvious disappointment in her voice.

I had been expecting a cake, but Lisa was delivering what looked like a giant cookie. My first thought—which I did not speak aloud—was, What happened? It did turn out to be a cake—but the flattest cake I'd ever seen.

And when Mom checked out the kitchen end of things, she found out why the cake never got past the bottom of the pan. Lisa had left out the baking powder. One ingredient was missing, and that made all the difference.

It could be the same in your life, especially as you face the new frontier of college. You could march into your future with most of the right ingredients—academic goals; positive attitude; things together with your family, your finances, and your friends—and life could still come out flat and you could go to bed a lot of nights feeling empty. You could be missing the one ingredient that makes all the difference.

Lisa's letters from college have repeatedly referred to that Ingredient—actually, that Relationship. For every new beginning in her life there has been one Person who has gone with her: Jesus Christ.

Jesus is the one Ingredient you can't do without. You may head into your future without your parents, your high school friends, your room, your boyfriend, your landmarks. But you need to go with Jesus in your heart.

The Bible refers to people who are "without hope and without God in the world" (Eph. 2:12). Actually, we're all without God unless we get rid of the wall between God and us. We've all felt that wall, but we're not sure why it's there.

It's like that husband and wife who were driving down the road, seated on opposite sides of the front seat. From the passenger side, the wife said, "Have you noticed that we don't sit close and cuddle like we used to?" To which her husband answered, "Well, I haven't moved."

God feels that way. He created us to live for Him, and we've lived for ourselves instead. In the words of the Bible, "Your iniquities have separated you from your God; your sins have hidden His face from you" (Isa. 59:2). We've moved away from God—He hasn't moved away from us. So we're lonely and no relationship seems to cure it because we're lonely for God. We're hurting because we're carrying pain He wants to share. We're empty because we have a hole in our soul only God can fill.

But there's this sin-wall—the accumulated distance of all the lies we ever told, the people we've ever hurt, the damaging words we ever spoke, the selfish things we ever said— all the sin of running our own lives.

Now, as you stand at the edge of your New World, is the time to get rid of the sin-wall between you and God, to be sure you enter every unknown with your hand in God's hand.

The same place in the Bible that described the "without God" problem doesn't stop there. It says, "But now in Christ Jesus you who once were far away have been brought near through the blood of Christ" (Eph. 2:13). When Jesus Christ died on that brutal cross, He was doing something about your God-wall—suffering the penalty for your sins, transferring all the guilt and hell of sin-living to Himself. The wall couldn't come down until the bill was paid, and Jesus paid it. You don't ever have to be far away from God again. You can be brought near.

Even though we moved away from God, He moved toward us. No one has ever loved you this much—He loved you so much "that He gave His one and only Son" so you may "have eternal life" (John 3:16). But like any love, it has to be responded to. One-way love won't work. John 3:16 says you have to believe in Him in order to get the forgiveness He paid for.

It's no accident that you have this book, or that you've read this far. God is reaching out to you right now. The most important question you could ask before you begin your future is, "How can I be sure I have this relationship with God?"

Let's get God's answer: "Repent, then, and turn to God, so that your sins may be wiped out [there goes the wall!], that times of refreshing may come from the Lord" (Acts 3:19). First, you have to turn away from running your own life. You have to tell God that you're ready to drop the junk. Then, with the junk gone, your hands will be free to grab Jesus and hold onto Him as your only hope—what it means to believe in Him.

You can open your life to God and His love right where you are. This isn't mere religion—it's Relationship, the Relationship you were made for. Jesus is yours for the inviting.

Not long ago I talked with a beautiful grandmother who is ninety-five years old. (Imagine your life plus seventy-five more years.) She's been through dozens of new beginnings, from leaving high school to rearing children to burying her husband to living in a wheelchair. But she has a glow and a smile that lights up a room.

I asked her what her favorite verse was in her well-worn Bible. She responded immediately, "Hebrews 13:8." Then, with a smile that made her look like a girl again, she quoted it—"Jesus Christ is the same yesterday and today and forever."

Her Jesus can be your Jesus. And He will be by your side through every change, every relationship, every crisis, and every need, and walk with you through life and one day into His presence. You'll need Him next year, and every year you live.

If Jesus has been the missing Person in your life, don't let Him be missing one more day. He's already moved in your direction—at the cross where He died for you. It's your move now.

Ron